How to Ma... from the ...

Fiona Macdonald

This book will tell you how to
make a Jumping Jack and an
Egyptian doll.

OXFORD

UNIVERSITY PRESS

OXFORD
UNIVERSITY PRESS

Great Clarendon Street, Oxford, OX2 6DP

Oxford University Press is a department of the University of Oxford.
It furthers the University's objective of excellence in research, scholarship,
and education by publishing worldwide in

Oxford New York

Athens Auckland Bangkok Bogotá Buenos Aires Cape Town Chennai
Dar es Salaam Delhi Florence Hong Kong Istanbul Karachi Kolkata
Kuala Lumpur Madrid Melbourne Mexico City Mumbai Nairobi Paris
São Paulo Shanghai Singapore Taipei Tokyo Toronto Warsaw

and associated companies in Berlin Ibadan

Oxford is a registered trade mark of Oxford University Press
in the UK and in certain other countries

Text © Fiona Macdonald 1999

The moral rights of the author have been asserted

Database right Oxford University Press (maker)

First published by Oxford University Press 1999
Reprinted 1999, 2001

A CIP record for this book is available from the British Library

ISBN 0 19 915594 1
Available in packs
Toys Pack of Six   (one of each book)   ISBN 0 19 915595 X
Toys Class Pack   (six of each book)   ISBN 0 19 915617 4

Printed in Hong Kong

Acknowledgements

The Publisher would like to thank the British Museum Egyptian
Department (p 4 *top*); and Robert Opie (p 10 *top*) for permission
to reproduce photographs

All other photography by Martin Sookias

With special thanks to Dr Richard Parkinson of the British Museum, and
the children and staff of St Barnabas School, Oxford, for their assistance.

Please note: the Ancient Egyptian figure used in this book was once
thought to be a doll for children, but it is now recognised to be a fertility
figurine placed in tombs. Examples of this type date to circa 2000BC and
mostly came from Thebes.

Contents

Dolls

This figure was made in Egypt. It is almost 4,000 years old.
It is made of wood and the hair is made of string and beads.

These dolls are made to look like the Egyptian figure. ▼

4

Materials and design

You will need these to make your doll.

wool

glue

felt-tip pen

hole punch

scissors

card

First, draw your doll on card.

head

arms

body

Making your doll

Next, cut out your doll.

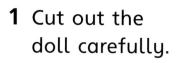

1 Cut out the doll carefully.

2 Cut pieces of wool for hair.

Now, fix the hair to
the doll's head.

3 Punch a hole
in the top of
the head. ▶

4 Thread a
piece of wool
through the
hole. ◀

5 Tie it round
all the other
pieces of wool. ▶

7

Decorating your doll

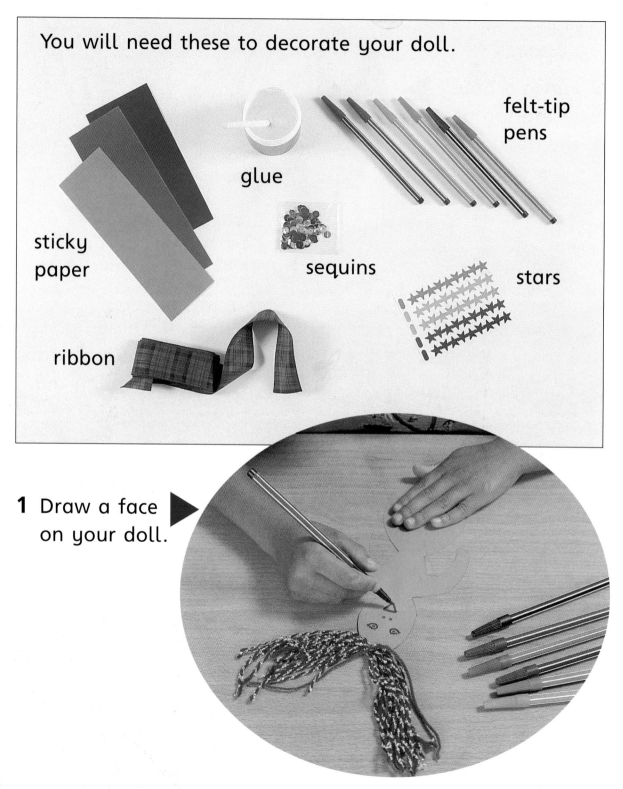

You will need these to decorate your doll.

felt-tip pens

glue

sticky paper

sequins

stars

ribbon

1 Draw a face on your doll. ▶

2 Draw patterns, and stick on ribbons and paper.

3 Stick on sequins or stars.

Jumping Jacks

This Jumping Jack ▶
was made in France.
It is about 200 years
old.

You can make a
Jumping Jack like this. ▼

Materials and design

You will need these to make your Jumping Jack.

wool

hole punch

paper fasteners

glue

felt-tip pens

card

stars

thin
string

sticky
paper

scissors

First, draw your Jumping Jack on card.

body

upper
legs

lower legs

Making the Jumping Jack

Next, cut out your Jumping Jack.

1 Cut out ▲ the pieces carefully, and decorate them. ▶

2 Punch eight holes to join the pieces together. ▼

3 Turn the pieces over. Put marks next to the holes with a red pen. ▶

4 Next, punch two more holes, and put marks next to them in green.

5 Join the legs together with paper fasteners. Push the paper fasteners through the red holes.

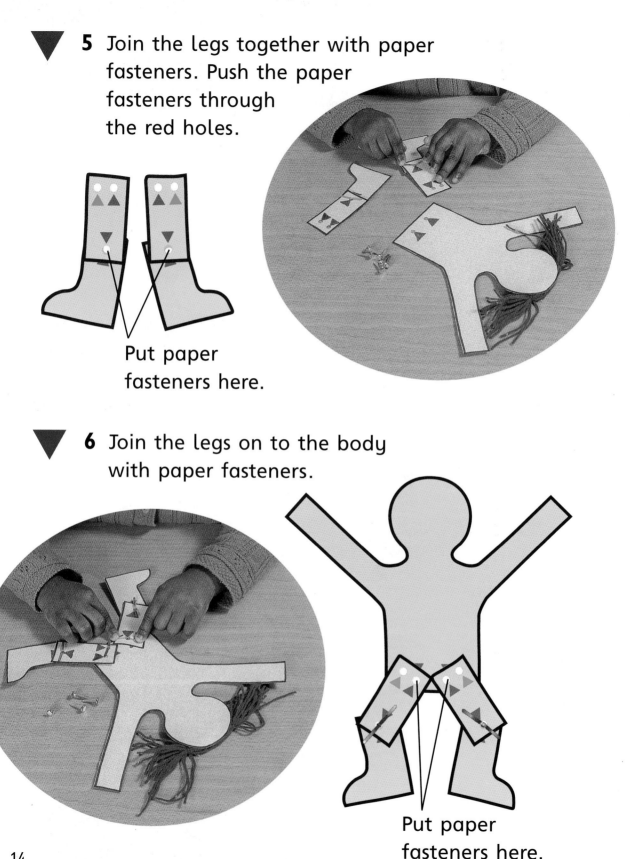

Put paper fasteners here.

6 Join the legs on to the body with paper fasteners.

Put paper fasteners here.

7 Thread a piece of string through the two green holes.

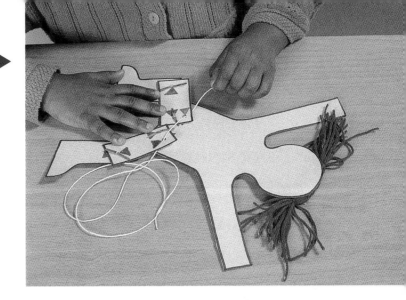

8 Tie the string in a big, loose loop with a long tail. Tie a double knot.

Finally, hold the body and pull the string up. Your Jumping Jack will jump!

a
b
c
d
e
f
g
h
i
j
k
l
m
n
o
p
q
r
s
t
u
v
w
x
y
z

Index